OCS Study
MMS 2005-034

Proceedings:

Beaufort Sea Polar Bear Monitoring Workshop

September 3-5, 2003
Anchorage, Alaska

By

Craig Perham
U.S. Fish and Wildlife Service
Marine Mammals Management
1011 E. Tudor Road
Anchorage, Alaska 99503

Prepared for:

U. S. Department of the Interior
Minerals Management Service
Alaska OCS Region
3801 Centerpoint Drive, Suite 500
Anchorage, Alaska 99503

Under Contract No. 2-4043-0053
Task Order No. AK-02-06

DISCLAIMER

CITATION

Suggested citation:

Perham, C.J. 2005. Proceedings of the Beaufort Sea Polar Bear Monitoring Workshop. OCS Study MMS 2005-034. Prepared by U.S. Fish and Wildlife Service-Marine Mammals Management, Anchorage, AK. Prepared for the U.S. Dept. of the Interior, Minerals Management Service, Alaska OCS Region, Anchorage, AK. 26 pp. plus appendices.

TABLE OF CONTENTS

EXECUTIVE SUMMARY

On September 3-5, 2003, the U.S. Fish and Wildlife Service (FWS) sponsored a workshop in Anchorage, Alaska. The goal of this meeting was to identify components for the development of a comprehensive, long-term polar bear monitoring program in association with the oil and gas industry in Alaska. This workshop was the initial effort to design an effective monitoring strategy that will provide information to help reduce bear/human interactions and help protect polar bear habitat for the Southern Beaufort Sea polar bear population. Potential oil and gas industry impacts on polar bears which were discussed during the workshop included: habitat alteration, chemical contamination, attraction and preclusion of areas, oil spills, industrial noise, and polar bear interactions with humans. Ideally, an improved management plan which identifies information necessary to monitor polar bears of the Southern Beaufort Sea stock will result from the recommendations of this workshop.

I. INTRODUCTION

In recent years, onshore and offshore oil and gas exploration and production operations in the Alaskan Beaufort Sea area have been increasing. Recent exploration activities, such as Northstar, Northwest Milne, McCovey, projects in the National Petroleum Reserve (NPR-A), and other prospects, indicate that North Slope oil and gas activities will continue into the future. Many of these new developments are occurring in the same habitat used by polar bears for denning, feeding, and seasonal movements.

Polar bears are a U.S. Fish and Wildlife Service (FWS) trust species protected by the Marine Mammal Protection Act (MMPA). The MMPA created a general moratorium on the 'take' of marine mammals and prohibitions for taking except when authorized. Incidental (unintentional) take of small numbers of marine mammals by U.S. citizens engaged in lawful activities (such as oil and gas exploration, development and production) may be authorized, but only through prescribed regulations and associated Letters of Authorization. The FWS is required to assess impacts of oil and gas development on polar bears every three to five years in order to issue regulations allowing unintentional, incidental take of polar bears, as detailed under Section 101(a)(5) of the MMPA of 1972. Take is defined as to "harass, hunt, capture, or kill, or attempt to harass, hunt, capture, or kill any marine mammal." The incidental take regulations are important to oil and gas operators because they provide a mechanism to minimize the likelihood of bear-human interactions which can lead to incidental takes of polar bears and address liability issues for incidental take.

In order to issue incidental take regulations, the FWS must: 1) receive a petition requesting promulgations of regulations; 2) evaluate the scope of activities; and 3) make a finding that activities have a negligible impact on polar bears, their habitat, and their availability for subsistence uses. The evaluation and findings process is similar to federal and state lease sale stipulations in environmental impact assessments for oil and gas operations which require an assessment of the potential environmental consequences of the planned activity.

Research on polar bears in Alaska conducted during the past 40 years has yielded valuable information regarding population ecology, den ecology, recruitment and survival, and habitat use by polar bears. However, quantitative data that specifically addresses potential cumulative impacts of development on polar bears and the effects of disturbance related to human activities on polar bear habitat use, as well as recruitment and survival, is lacking. In the past, potential impacts from specified activities have been monitored on a case-by-case basis. Currently, long term monitoring programs do not exist to monitor cumulative effects on polar bears in the Beaufort Sea. A comprehensive, fully integrated monitoring approach to assess the potential effects of oil and gas development on polar bears is warranted. The development of a long-term monitoring program will help to increase the accuracy and adequately assess these potential impacts and effects, and to implement measures to minimize impacts.

II. BACKGROUND INFORMATION

THE INCIDENTAL TAKE REGULATION AND MONITORING PROCESS

The MMPA prohibits "take" of any marine mammal. Exceptions to the prohibition of taking marine mammals include: 1) subsistence hunting, 2) scientific research, 3) public display, 4) incidental take, 5) intentional take, and 6) defense of life. Oil and gas industry activities are authorized to take small numbers of polar bears using incidental and intentional take exemptions. The FWS considers an incidental take to be an infrequent, unavoidable, or accidental event, which alters the behavior or movement of a bear. The FWS has historically defined, "harass," as any action that results in an observable change in the behavior of a marine mammal, such as an abrupt termination of breeding or feeding, or avoidance behavior. Currently, the term, "harass" has been re-defined as: "any act that either disturbs or is likely to disturb a marine mammal's natural behavioral patterns to a point where the patterns are abandoned or significantly altered or is directed towards a specific individual or group and is likely to cause disturbance by disrupting natural behavior."

Authority for developing regulations is provided through the MMPA. Regulations allow U.S. citizens to take small numbers of polar bears incidental to specified activities and a specified region provided that:
1. Total take will have a negligible impact on the population. A negligible impact is defined as an impact resulting from the specified activity (oil and gas) that cannot be reasonably (not extreme or excessive) expected to, and is not reasonably likely to, adversely affect the species or stock through effects on annual rates of recruitment or survival.
2. Take will not affect the availability of the species for subsistence users.

It should be noted that incidental take authorizations do not permit industrial activities, rather, they allow for an exemption from the take provisions of the MMPA while specified activities are being conducted.

The regulation process begins with a petition from a U.S. citizen to incidentally take polar bears during certain activities (in this case, oil and gas activities). Submitted petition components include: 1) operations to be conducted; 2) dates and region of activities; 3) species of concern, the number and type of anticipated take; 4) anticipated impact on species, habitat, and subsistence use; and 5) mitigation measures.

An environmental assessment is written to evaluate the effect that this Federal Action (issuing regulations) may have on the resources. Next, the FWS must determine whether impacts of incidental takes are significant to the affected polar bear population. Finally, if warranted, a Finding of No Significant Impact (FONSI) is generated if the FWS concludes that the current action will have a negligible impact on the recruitment and survival of polar bears, as well as no unmitigable impact for subsistence uses. A public comment period occurs during the draft regulations. If the FONSI is accepted, then incidental take regulations are issued for up to a five year period.

Once regulations are in place, oil and gas operators can apply for an incidental take exemption by requesting a Letter of Authorization (LOA) from the FWS for specified activities, including exploration, development, and production activities. Exploration activities include winter seismic surveys and open-water seismic and shallow hazards surveys. Development activities include road construction, pipeline construction, camp construction, transportation, demobilization, restoration, and remediation. Production activities include the daily operation of production fields, such as the maintenance of facilities and operational improvements to the fields.

In order for the FWS to issue a LOA, the operator must provide information on the activity to be conducted, the location of the activity, the time frame of the activity, a polar bear encounter/human interaction plan, a plan of cooperation with affected subsistence villages that considers the impact of the activity on subsistence harvest of polar bears, and a polar bear monitoring plan. The FWS and the operator typically meet to discuss polar bear monitoring requirements. The LOA requires that monitoring results must be reported to FWS within three months after the activity has been concluded.

The purpose of monitoring and reporting requirements is to assess the effects of industrial activities on polar bears to ensure that take is minimal to the polar bear population, and to detect any unanticipated effects of take. The monitoring focus can be site specific, area specific, or population specific. Site-specific monitoring measures bear-human encounter rates, outcomes of encounters, and trends of bear activity in the industrial areas, such as bear numbers, activity, and seasonal use. Area-specific monitoring includes analyzing polar bear spatial and temporal use trends, sex/age composition, and risk assessment to unpredictable events, such as oil spills. Population-specific monitoring includes investigating polar bear life history parameters, such as recruitment, survival, physical condition, status, and mortality.

Since the inception of the incidental take regulations for the Beaufort Sea in 1993, the FWS has required monitoring for industrial activities. To determine whether cumulative impacts from activities are adversely affecting polar bears, a long-term monitoring strategy is necessary to detect and measure changes in the status of the polar bear population over time.

The objectives of a long-term monitoring strategy are to:
1) identify information necessary to reliably assess possible direct and indirect effects of oil and gas activities on polar bears;
2) develop research studies necessary to obtain this information;
3) identify measures that could be taken to avoid or mitigate the adverse effects of oil and gas activities;
4) identify the resources (time, money, special equipment) necessary to accomplish these objectives.

III. WORKSHOP OBJECTIVES AND METHODS

In September 2003, the FWS hosted a workshop to identify the elements necessary to develop a comprehensive monitoring program to better address potential short and long-term impacts of oil and gas development on polar bears in Alaska, particularly the Southern Beaufort Sea population. Specifically, the objectives of this workshop were to identify elements necessary to: 1) help reduce bear/human interactions, and 2) help protect polar bear habitat for the Southern Beaufort Sea polar bear population.

The workshop was held at the Hilltop Ski Area Lodge, Anchorage, Alaska on September 3-5, 2003. Participants included government agency representatives from FWS, U.S. Geological Survey (USGS), Alaska Department of Fish and Game (ADFG), Canada's Northwest Territories Department of Resources, Wildlife, and Economic Development, Minerals Management Service (MMS), U.S. Air Force, and U.S. Department of Interior; oil and gas industry representatives from EnCana Corporation, BP Exploration (Alaska), Inc., ConocoPhillips Alaska, Inc., and Western GeCo; consultants from Lynx Enterprises, OASIS Environmental, and West, Inc.; non-government organizations (NGO) representatives from the Audubon Society, Arctic Connections, Polar Bears International, and Defenders of Wildlife; and the University of Alberta.

The first day of the workshop featured presentations including the natural history of polar bears inhabiting the Southern Beaufort Sea, mitigation tools from recent research efforts, and a history of the incidental take and monitoring process. During the remainder of the workshop, participants were involved in working group sessions where a list of possible effects of oil and gas activities on polar bears were identified and discussed. These included: habitat alteration, chemical contamination, oil spills, industrial noise, attraction to human activity, preclusion of habitat use, and human/polar bear interactions. Participants then identified potential research and monitoring needs related to the list of effects, using the following questions as guidelines:

1) What do we know about the effects of oil and gas activities on polar bears?
    Summarized in the Proceedings under subsections, *Potential Impacts*.
2) What is the most current information available regarding this effect?
3) What types of information/data are needed to more accurately monitor and evaluate impacts of this effect?
    Questions 2 and 3 are summarized in the Proceedings under subsections, *Monitoring*, for individual impacts.
4) How can monitoring for these effects be improved?
    Summarized in the Proceedings under subsections, *Recommendations*, for individual impacts.

This report summarizes the topics of the workshop discussions regarding the identified impacts. It also presents a draft strategy, in matrix form, listing the tasks of a long-term approach to monitoring the effects of industrial activities on polar bears.

IV. DISCUSSION

A. EXISTING POLAR BEAR RESEARCH, MONITORING, MITIGATION PROGRAMS

Initially, workshop participants identified recent (within 5 years) and ongoing research efforts pertinent to polar bears conducted by the FWS, USGS, and consultants in the Beaufort Sea. These include:

1. Recording the distribution of maternal polar bear dens in the arctic environment;
2. Real-time tissue contaminants analysis of Beaufort Sea polar bears monitoring levels of organochlorines, heavy metal, and other compounds;
3. Population estimation studies of Beaufort Sea polar bears (mark/recapture; population parameters, such as recruitment and survival);
4. Polar bear habitat resource selection (sea ice vs. terrestrial den habitat);
5. Polar bear whale carcass feeding ecology study;
6. Acoustic monitoring of industrial noise and vibrations at maternal polar bear den sites;
7. Use of FLIR imagery to detect polar bear maternal dens;
8. Oil spill modeling;
9. Polar bear population range boundary delineation (i.e., mapping out the area used by polar bears);
10. Polar bear den site behavior at emergence;
11. Arctic Nearshore Impact Monitoring in the Developed Area (ANIMIDA);
12. Polar bear movement studies (observing seasonal movement patterns through telemetry); and
13. Verification of maternal polar bear dens using scent-trained dogs.

In addition, workshop participants identified existing monitoring programs that have been, or are currently in place, and provide information pertinent to polar bear monitoring in relation to oil and gas activities on the North Slope. They include:

1. The FWS polar bear observation form;
2. Fall coastal polar bear aerial surveys;
3. Trained marine mammal observers associated with long-term field operations, such as seismic and transport activities;
4. Ice monitoring for offshore oil and gas operations in the oilfield units;
5. Weather monitoring;
6. Polar bear subsistence harvest monitoring;
7. Ringed seal on-ice aerial surveys and monitoring (Northstar Before After Control Impact (BACI) study and ADFG aerial surveys);
8. Polar bear tissue archiving: Arctic Marine Monitoring and Trends Assessment Program (AMMTAP);
9. Known polar bear den monitoring by agencies and industry;
10. Bowhead whale physiology data based on harvest information from ADFG;
11. Circumpolar contaminant studies, monitoring polar bear contaminant levels;
12. Bowhead carcass monitoring data for polar bears from National Marine Fisheries Service (NMFS) bowhead whale surveys;
13. ANIMIDA;

14. GIS of offshore industry activities from the MMS Human Activities Database;
15. Alaska Department of Environmental Conservation (DEC) oil spill database;
16. National Ice Data Base;
17. North Slope Borough (NSB) community polar bear patrols;
18. Aerial photographs of the north slope terrestrial habitat (ConocoPhillips, BPXA, DOI, DOD, DNR, etc.) and
19. Arctic Borderlands program, monitoring climate change.

Workshop participants also compiled a list of existing mitigation and management techniques, which include:
1. Industry Letters of Authorization authorized by the FWS;
2. Industry-generated polar bear interaction plans;
3. The use of FLIR imagery to detect polar bear maternal dens;
4. The 1-mile buffer around known maternal polar bear dens;
5. Timing restrictions for industrial activities near known maternal polar bear dens;
6. Trained marine mammal observers;
7. North Slope industry polar bear hazing program within the oil and gas fields;
8. North Slope Information and Education Program (polar bear awareness and deterrence training);
9. Arctic National Wildlife Refuge as a refugium, where the policy mandate protects polar bears and their habitat;
10. The FWS Polar Bear Habitat Conservation Strategy;
11. Leasing process (oil lease sale stipulations for minimizing polar bear/human interactions);
12. Verification of maternal polar bear dens using scent-trained dogs;
13. NSB community polar bear patrols; and
14. Abandoned industrial facilities as potential denning habitat.

B. HABITAT ALTERATION

Potential Impacts

Habitat alteration describes potential changes in the physical habitat used by polar bears in the Beaufort Sea caused by anthropogenic activities, such as increased human development and climate change. Three main habitat types which bears use could be impacted: 1) sea ice marine environment; 2) terrestrial denning habitat; and 3) coastal habitat during open-water season. Habitat changes could be manifested in the destruction, degradation, modification, or creation of habitat.

Sea Ice
Effects from human-induced habitat alteration on sea ice or the marine environment can occur within hours, such as an oil spill, or can be long-term, such as climate change. Sea ice will be the most apparent habitat affected by climate change. Although the warming of the earth's atmosphere by climate change is a world-wide phenomenon, it was discussed as an anthropogenic effect that could alter polar bear habitat because seasonal changes, such as extended duration of open water, may preclude sea ice habitat use by

restricting some bears to coastal areas. The reduction of sea ice extent, caused by climate change, may also affect the timing of polar bear seasonal movements between the coastal regions and the pack ice. If the sea ice continues to recede as predicted, it is hypothesized that polar bears may spend more time on land rather than on sea ice, as seen in the Hudson Bay. The challenge in the Beaufort Sea will be predicting changes in ice habitat, barrier islands, and coastal habitats in relation to changes in polar bear distribution and use of habitat.

Denning Habitat
Polar bears use both ice and terrestrial habitat for denning in the Southern Beaufort Sea. Expansion of the oil and gas fields throughout the North Slope and its ability to alter maternal polar bear den locations to due potential disturbance was classified as a potential impact. Although terrestrial change to the arctic environment has included the reduction in size of industrial footprints, the cumulative impacts associated with more facilities spread out over a larger area was a concern discussed by participants.

Coastal Habitat
Beaufort Sea coastal habitat is most important to polar bears during maternal denning (October to April). One of the potential effects of industrial activity to coastal environments has been habitat alteration through the development of infrastructure. The cumulative effect of increased multiple industrial footprints was also discussed in relation to coastal habitat as well.

Another us of coastal habitat for polar bears is as a travel corridor. The majority of polar bear movement and use of the coastline, including the developed areas, occurs during the fall and spring of the year. Similarly, polar bears often use natural and man-made areas to rest along the coast, such as facilities: docks, breakwaters, islands, and other structures. These structures usually extend out from the nearshore environment several miles, such as the Saltwater Treatment Plant (STP) at the end of the West Dock causeway or the Endicott causeway. Bears have been known to spend days on these spots resting. This use occurs generally after bears swim in from the pack ice to land during late summer and fall months. Bears that become stranded on land, or choose to remain when the ice pulls away can also spend more time resting than bears on the pack ice, thereby conserving energy. It is uncertain if the bears deliberately go to these areas because of certain attractions or are randomly heading toward land and make for the closest point.

In regards to human/bear interactions, these coastal areas are important to industry from a safety standpoint and to the bears from an energetic standpoint. Views from workshop participants regarding these "rest areas" were varied. Some felt it was necessary to keep the bears moving if they make land at an operational facility through deterrent activities to minimize human/bear interactions. Other participants felt food-stressed bears need to rest after a long swim from open water.

Coastal habitat can also be altered by placement of facilities. For example, once placed on a prospect, exploration drill ships, such as the SDC (recently used for EnCana on the McCovey prospect), can create artificial downstream leads in the ice depending on how the ship is placed. These leads can attract ringed seals (*Phoca hispida*) and possibly polar bears. One concern expressed by participants questioned whether industry could be attracting bears artificially due to the placement of facilities, thereby potentially increasing the risk of exposure in the event of an oil spill.

Monitoring Habitat Alteration

The primary focus of current polar bear monitoring is the protection of denning females and maternal denning habitat. Current mitigation, management stipulations, and regulations regarding polar bear denning habitat were questioned by participants in terms of their effectiveness. Most notable was the one-mile buffer FWS places around known maternal dens to limit disturbances caused by activity. The distance of one mile was originally an arbitrary condition set back in the 1970s. Some participants felt this was a conservative distance. The FWS has felt comfortable with this size of buffer and the type of mitigation within this buffer was conducted on a case by case basis. Extenuating circumstances may warrant modification of the timing of activities with the one-mile buffer, reduction of the size of the buffer, or enhanced monitoring requirements. Mitigation could also be a restriction of all activities within the buffer, added marine mammal observers monitoring activity within the buffer, or a cessation of activities in the buffer until after the female bear emerges from the den.

In an effort to investigate disturbance distances, a recent study of industrial noise and vibration measured certain attenuation distances of various industrial sounds from artificial polar bear dens. This study found that industrial noises could be received in dens from as far as 500 meters in distance. In addition, a polar bear den emergence study is currently investigating disturbance effects on recently emerged polar bears. Currently, the FWS does not have data on levels of disturbance effects on polar bears at various distances or at different times of the denning period.

In addition to the one-mile buffer around polar bear dens, other mitigation stipulations include: 1) limit activities in the den buffer until after the bear emerges, essentially avoiding the denning period; and 2) use polar bear denning habitat maps to avoid denning areas during the planning stages of a proposed project. These mitigation techniques appear to be effective as there have been no known den abandonment due to industrial activities since these stipulations were instituted.

Participants discussed the value of the coastal areas of the Arctic National Wildlife Refuge (Arctic Refuge) as a refugium for polar bears, particularly in the future under a reduced sea ice scenario caused by climate change. This is due to its status as a national wildlife refuge with its exclusion of oil and gas activities. In the Arctic Refuge, there is a perceived lower threshold for habitat alteration as human-caused habitat modification is currently deemed incompatible with the purpose for establishing the refuge. On-going monitoring activities in the refuge need to be identified. Natural changes of the habitat may be documented through aerial photography and ground-truthing. With that in mind, participants questioned if there were different monitoring standards between the developed areas, such as the oilfields, and undeveloped areas, such as the Arctic Refuge.

8

Participants further discussed the value of polar bear habitats. A quantitative value could be placed on different habitat types to improve monitor changes. For denning habitat a distribution of known dens in the denning areas may serve as an example to help pinpoint valuable, preferred denning habitat. A comprehensive slope-wide map of potential denning habitat, coupled with a probability model of likelihood based on historic denning records would help when investigating small scale areas, such as specific oil lease areas.

Participants also discussed whether coastal denning or resting areas would be positively or negatively affected by the expanding industrial landscape. Negative effects could include avoidance of potential resting or denning sites near industrial areas, such as roads, pipelines, staging areas, pads, and the larger production facilities. Positive effects could include use of elevated staging pads as dens sites. For example, polar bear den sites have occurred on an abandoned gravel staging pad within the Prudhoe Bay operations area and on a gravel runway ramp at the Bullen Point Long Range Radar Site near the Badami production site. Questions that arose during this discussion included: Could artificial substrate add to natural denning habitat if that habitat is limiting? Will limitation of denning habitat near industry be an issue in the future?

Participants further discussed the value of polar bear habitats. A quantitative value could be placed on different habitat types to better monitor changes. For denning habitat a distribution of known dens in the denning areas may serve as an example to help pinpoint valuable, preferred denning habitat. A comprehensive map of potential denning habitat slope-wide, coupled with a probability model of likelihood based on historic denning records would help when investigating small scale areas, such as specific oil lease areas.

Although some records document the cumulative expansion of the oil and gas industry over the Arctic Coastal Plain, participants discussed ways to more accurately record future physical changes to habitat from industrial expansion. This would entail monitoring and documenting habitat changes that may affect polar bears. Monitoring areas in the early stages of development, such as NPR-A, would be important. GIS coverages and aerial photographs of the industrial footprints in new areas that are current and available to agencies, as well as current coverages of the habitat may be tools to aid in the monitoring habitat alteration. This habitat monitoring program could be combined with polar bear telemetry data, and/or denning data to examine alteration affects on bears.

Habitat Alteration Recommendations
1. Document naturally-occurring changes of the physical habitat over time, such as the erosion of barrier islands and loss of sea ice habitat.
2. Document any physical changes to habitat due to the increased development of oilfield infrastructure.
3. Identify important polar bear use areas, i.e. "movement corridors, resting areas, denning habitat," across the Arctic coast.
4. Consider the value of abandoned infrastructure for denning or resting habitat.
5. Complete denning habitat maps for NPR-A and Arctic Refuge.

6. Consider research to document and possibly develop a predictive model measuring the use of one denning substrate over another (Sea ice vs. terrestrial maternal denning habitat).
7. Document impacts related to arctic climate change.

C. CONTAMINANTS

Potential Impacts

This section addresses contaminants and sources other than oil and oil derivatives. Oil is addressed separately in this report. Polar bears can consume contaminants directly, such as consumption of ethylene glycol, or indirectly through consumption of contaminated food and water containing organochlorines and trace elements. Workshop participants spent minimal time discussing contamination because current studies suggest low levels of most contaminants that could affect polar bears occur within the North Slope environment.

Monitoring Contaminants

Monitoring for contaminant levels in the environment and in the Southern Beaufort Sea polar bear population is ongoing through a variety of Arctic studies. Contaminant levels come from both anthropogenic and natural sources. Further clarification of contaminant levels in polar bears, prey species and the environment is necessary to fully understand the impacts of contaminants on polar bears and the Arctic environment in the Beaufort Sea.

The FWS polar bear bio-monitoring program, which investigates contaminant levels in harvested polar bears, and the USGS-managed Arctic Marine Monitoring and Trends Assessment Program (AMMTAP) Program, which archives tissue samples from harvested or stranded animals for future analysis, are two projects that address contaminant monitoring goals. The FWS has recently completed two reports summarizing concentrations of organochlorines and metals from adult male polar bears harvested from the Southern Beaufort Sea and Chukchi/Bering Sea populations. Contaminant samples have also been archived with AMMTAP for future analyses of new compounds and for development of spatial and temporal contaminant trends.

Other projects, such as the Arctic Nearshore Impact Monitoring in Development Areas (ANIMIDA), a MMS-funded project, investigating baseline data of anthropogenic contamination in the nearshore ocean environment in Stefansson Sound of the Beaufort Sea, will indirectly benefit polar bear monitoring programs by assessing contaminant levels in the Arctic environment. In addition, current sampling requirements for air discharge of oil and gas facilities appears to be adequate.

Contaminant discussion centered on improving current monitoring efforts through increased coordination and long-term funding of existing programs. Program samples need to be systematically collected and analysis needs to consider synergistic effects. Variation in bear movement or feeding patterns may also reflect differential accumulation of contaminants. Several approaches to address such issues were discussed. They included the possibility of polar bear hair or scat collection in evaluating individual contaminant variation over time or developing a regional approach that measures "before/after" contamination levels near developed areas, such as Northstar.

Contaminants Recommendations

1. Continue contaminant monitoring programs, such as AMMTAP and ANIMIDA, and conduct rigorous analysis of the data to allow for analysis of compounding effects, e.g., variation in bear feeding patterns. Improve sampling protocols and study designs to ensure systematic sampling.
2. Analyze specimens and report results in a timely fashion.
3. Stabilize funding for the AMMTAP program.
4. Monitor disease and parasites in polar bears. Evaluate the trend in relation to climate change.
5. Develop a regional "before/after" contaminant monitoring approach in relation to industry development, where possible.

D. ATTRACTION/AVOIDANCE

Potential Impacts

Polar bears may be attracted to industrial facilities and activities by smells, sounds, or sights. They may be precluded from denning and resting areas due to industrial activities as discussed in the "Habitat Alteration" Section.

Three North Slope attractants were identified and discussed: 1) garbage; 2) whale carcass sites; and 3) lights. Improvements to the polar bear observation form in terms of attractants information was also discussed.

Garbage
Even though great strides have been implemented for reducing the attraction of garbage and kitchen wastes at facilities and camps slope-wide, participants identified this as a persistent attractant problem that can be properly managed through increased vigilance. New policies regarding the installation and placement of bear-proof garbage cans and the establishment of an electric fence around the NSB dump appear to have reduced the number of polar bear encounters caused by food wastes.

Whale Carcass Sites
Cross Island, Barrow, and Kaktovik were identified as areas that have the potential to attract polar bears due to the presence of hunter-harvested bowhead whale (*Balaena mysticetus*) remains. Participants had particular concerns regarding Cross Island, due to its close location to the oil and gas fields, including whether congregations of bears at Cross Island increases the number of polar bears moving through the oilfield. Participants also discussed whether whale carcasses were considered a natural or a human-induced food source, and recognized that, regardless, more control over the

carcass sites may be necessary to limit polar bear-human interactions within the North Slope area. Whale carcasses attract large numbers of bears to these sites during the fall open-water season. Because these bear aggregations affect bear distribution, these areas could increase the bear's susceptibility to oil spills, disease transmission, and could increase their presence in the oilfield as they transit to and from these areas, especially Cross Island. Some participants thought that the presence of carcasses at Cross Island might decrease the presence of polar bears in the oilfield because it may deter some bears from coming onshore. Participants discussed the removal of the carcasses at these sites. One option, pushing carcasses off the island into the sea, may cause the carcasses to float to less desirable locations, such as the developed coastline where industrial infrastructure is located. The consensus of the group was to develop a solution with the local whalers, the NMFS, FWS, MMS, and industry that would limit polar bear-human interactions, possibly by seasonally removing or burying the whale remains. This would require considerable planning and will have to be a joint effort between these various groups. Monitoring of the carcass sites is currently being studied by the FWS with funding from the MMS; a final report is due in 2005.

In addition, there is a small but increasing tourism industry for polar bear viewing that is emerging in relation to the bowhead whale carcass sites at Barrow and Kaktovik. A major concern among the participants was the sanctioning of such an industry based on a human-induced food source. Participants were also concerned that if the tourism industry was sanctioned, tourism development would not outpace bear viewing regulations. This concern is particularly important for Kaktovik because its carcass site is located near town. Participants acknowledged that villages, government officials (borough, city and tribal), and the FWS need to understand the changing tourism dynamics in relation to bear viewing because once patterns of bear-human interaction are set, they are hard to change. Furthermore, if tourism based on polar bear viewing at whale carcass sites becomes popular and economically significant, it will be difficult to manage and it may conflict with suggested plans to dispose of the carcasses slope-wide if protocols are not in place prior to bear viewing opportunities. Consequently, the local governments and the FWS need to address the bear viewing issue in terms of the trade-offs between the economic return to the community versus safety issues for its inhabitants. Workshop participants agreed that the local communities need to take the lead in the development of bear safety guidelines and bear viewing protocols. The FWS would offer guidance and technical support to a management plan initiated by the local communities.

Lights
Facility lights were identified as a potential attractant for polar bears. Lights are used for visibility at facilities and detection of polar bears. Based on a study in Canada, bears were not attracted to areas lit with high intensity lights. Consequently, high intensity lights were installed in certain areas on the North Slope; however, polar bears did not seem to be affected one way or the other by them.

Levels of lighting and types of light (i.e., flashing) may affect Industry monitoring practices for polar bear observations. In some instances, strobe lights used to prevent bird strikes, for example, make it difficult to see bears in the distance. In addition, current facility lighting plans suggest extending illumination further off-pad so the initial observation of a bear is further from the pad.

Monitoring Attraction/Avoidance

<u>Polar bear observation form</u>
Industry uses a polar bear observation form to document all sightings of polar bears. This form is used to monitor bear sightings across the North Slope. Two points discussed included clearly defining the "attractions" block on the observation form so this information could be more useful. Secondly, participants discussed refining the observation form to describe the animal's behavior and movement as it pertains to attraction or avoidance (towards/away from site).

<u>Habitat Restoration</u>
Participants noted that prior to the restoration or remediation of abandoned facilities or the removal of gravel pads, FWS should consider their value as potential den habitat for polar bears as some bears appear to be attracted to certain areas. For example, bears have been known to den in snowdrifts on human-created substrate. During the winter of 2002-2003, a polar bear denned in a snowdrift created by the Bullen Point Long Range Radar Site runway ramp. Polar bears have also used, or explored an abandoned gravel staging pad located on the coast between Milne Point and Beechey Point as a denning area for multiple years. Participants suggested that certain man-made sites may be more valuable as bear habitat than being restored to natural conditions.

Attraction/Avoidance Recommendations
1. Examine the known data, such as movement data from collared animals, for trends of polar bear movement from the bowhead whale carcass sites to the oil fields.
2. Conduct meetings with FWS, MMS, NOAA, industry representatives, the Eskimo Whaling Commission, and local governments to discuss the future of the whale carcass sites.
3. Define "attractants" on the polar bear observation form.
4. Change the polar bear observation form to describe bear behavior in terms of attraction and avoidance, using a simple map of the area.
5. Obtain industry maps coverages (GIS) and use them to plot current polar bear locations and movement in and around facilities.
6. Compare the use of denning on human-created substrates to the use of the surrounding, suitable naturally occurring areas.
7. Monitor the annual numbers of polar bear viewing tourists and guides.

<u>E. OIL SPILLS</u>

Potential Impacts

The discharge of oil into the environment could directly affect polar bears through external contact with oil, or through ingestion. Spills can occur on water, on ice, or on land. Oil ingestion by polar bears could occur through consumption of contaminated prey, grooming, or inhalation of vapors and exposure to certain levels of oil appear to be lethal to polar bears.

Oil spills can also have indirect effects on polar bears as well. For example, a decrease in ringed seal (the main food source of polar bears) numbers, could affect the distribution of polar bears in local areas. Scavenging dead seals, oiled from a spill, could also increase hydrocarbon exposure to polar bears. In addition, an offshore oil spill could cause a local depletion of seal prey items (i.e., fish and invertebrates) resulting in dispersal of seals away from the nearshore area. This, in turn, would affect polar bear movements as they would have to move to other areas in search of food. While searching for seals polar bears may come in contact with nearshore and coastal oilfield facilities, which could potentially increase polar bear/human interactions.

Monitoring Oil Spills

Oil spill monitoring and research in the Beaufort Sea has concentrated on risk assessments analysis, such as oil spill modeling. Oil spill models have been developed in the past for various offshore oil and gas projects, but participants felt they need to be updated. One way to improve models would be to combine polar bear sightings to a population level assessment, where observations could be converted into probabilities. MMS has also created a predicative oil spill model, but it is limited to nearshore application. In addition, industry can incorporate polar bear scenarios into their spill drill models to practice deterrence and other procedures that may be necessary if a spill occurs.

Oil Spill Recommendations

1. Improve the precision of oil spill modeling.
2. Update oil spill models, i.e., including new developments into the models, etc.
3. Develop and incorporate polar bear scenarios within the North Slope regional spill drills to help in field testing of operational techniques.
4. Update FWS Oil Spill Response Plan.

F. INDUSTRIAL NOISE

Potential Impacts

Noise can affect polar bear use of various habitats. Industrial noise disturbance can originate from either stationary or moving sources. Examples of stationary sources include coastal production facilities, or production facilities located on offshore islands, and exploratory drilling. Examples of moving sources include vessel and aircraft traffic, open-water seismic and ice-covered (vibroseis) exploration, ice-road construction and associated vehicle traffic.

Monitoring Industrial Noise

Noise transmission is variable; it depends on temperature/weather characteristics, substrate, and ambient noise levels. Bear reactions to noise are also variable and may depend on whether a bear is denning or moving through an area. For example, bears react differently to the same sounds depending on the situation (i.e., if a bear has been chased by a snow machine then it may react more strongly to snow machine noise). Although it is widely held that female polar bears may be more susceptible to noise when they emerge from dens, most bears habituate fairly rapidly to noise. In general, bears habituate to sounds when they occur without other associated stimuli.

Currently, there is no direct monitoring of industrial noise in relation to the effects on polar bears. Sound disturbance is mitigated through the 1-mile buffer placed on known bear dens, and the potential "cease work" requirement during the denning period. Two studies on the North Slope have contributed to our understanding of noise effects on polar bears. Both studies investigated noise levels received in artificial polar bear dens. A study conducted in the late 1980s by Blix and Lentfer (published in the journal, *Arctic*, in 1992, volume 45/1) concluded that, in general, vibroseis machines and helicopters were inaudible above the background noise if greater than 100m from these noises. At Flaxman Island in 2002, a study to determine industrial noise and vibration attenuation concluded that; 1) snow is a good insulator for sound; and 2) the maximum distance vehicle noise was detected above background noise in dens ranged from 500m to 2000m.

Although these two studies have contributed to our understanding of noise received in dens, there is a lack of scientific knowledge on the hearing range of polar bears and the direct effect of noise on polar bears. A dedicated research project investigating the hearing range of polar bears coupled with a study to evaluate measured effects on polar bears would be the next step in answering questions regarding industrial noise.

Industrial Noise Recommendations

1. Design a study that can accurately test disturbance effects such as heart rate or movement on bears in dens, rather than by indirect means, such as acoustic measurements.
2. Revisit the one-mile buffer requirement around maternal polar bear dens to determine whether the distance is appropriate.
3. Reassess den mitigation practices – monitor the den, rather than mitigate around industrial activities.

G. POLAR BEAR/HUMAN INTERACTIONS

Potential Impacts

Polar bear encounters with humans can result in the harassment or death of the bear and injury or death to humans. Polar bears are most likely to encounter humans on the Beaufort Sea coastline during the fall (late August to mid October) and spring (March to May) periods of the year, when bears are found on the land-fast ice and along the coastline.

Monitoring Polar Bear/Human Interactions

Existing tools for monitoring and minimizing polar bear/human interactions are: 1) LOAs for incidental and intentional take; 2) outreach /education programs; 3) Industry-sponsored polar bear/human interaction plans; 4) facility site plans; 5) safety training, posters, signs; and 6) deterrent programs (i.e., hazing).

Information Services
Participants discussed various ways the FWS could prevent and limit polar bear/human interactions and improve monitoring programs and data gathering.

FWS North Slope field office
Participants felt that FWS should increase its presence in the oilfield by staffing a year-round or seasonal office in the Prudhoe Bay-Deadhorse area. This would allow for a more accessible resource to support FWS incidental and intentional take programs, as well as encourage additional participation with other agency cooperators, such as FWS-subsistence, MMS, and ADFG.

Website
In addition to a North Slope field office, posting information on a polar bear monitoring web site was discussed as a mechanism to share and receive various polar bear information with interested parties. A website could be an inexpensive method to post summary information. This information could include natural history; bear behavior, hazing information, bear sightings in the oilfields, regulations, reporting forms, etc.

Polar Bear Observation Form
Workshop participants discussed the importance of clear objectives for the polar bear observation program and form: documenting take, movements of bears, behaviors of bears in the oilfield, etc. Some thought that the form does not describe long-term observations accurately and that there is a big variance in reporting deterrence. Originally, the form was to document take; the information was used to evaluate if a take did occur. However, if the FWS objectives have changed, the form needs to modify accordingly and operators need to be informed of these changes.

Participants discussed at length how to improve the polar bear observation form, i.e., to make it easier to fill out. There was consensus on improving the observation form because it is a useful, low cost method to gather polar bear/oilfield information. Participants also agreed that there is a need for consistency in data collection. Information collected has to be as consistent and complete as the possible. Historically, some observation forms were very detailed, while others were missing data. Various suggestions for improvement of the form included:

1. Keep observation form to one page;
2. Include reference pictures of polar bears to accurately classify age classes
3. Follow the Keep It Simple Rule – have boxes to check or lists to circle, for characterizing polar bear movement data and distance components, habitat type, and bear behavior;
4. Have observers use maps of areas or facilities, where possible, to map bear location and movements;

5. Emphasize the importance of bear locations, possibly using a GPS and/or provided rangefinder binoculars to provide a basis for spatial analysis;
6. Simplify weather to visibility criteria. Use wind speed: light, moderate, or strong;

7. Observers could photograph bears to classify physical traits or age class, but may not be necessary as a requirement on the form;
8. FWS could eventually create an electronic web based observation form;
9. Describe repeat polar bear observations on the form so observations are not double counted;
10. Describe deterrence events as easy, moderate, or difficult to deter the bear.
11. Clarify the type of take on the form, when it occurred, under what conditions it occurred, and if human activity had any effect.
12. Finally, a draft of the new polar bear observation form should be reviewed by key security staff before it is implemented as oilfield security will be the primary observers.

Reporting and Training
Participants felt that training videos, slide shows and FWS-sponsored presentations have been effective; however, the FWS needs to provide feedback to field people submitting observation forms. Reports of bear activity should have a direct follow-up with the observers to gather more information. Additionally, feedback could be general or it could be site-specific for each oilfield unit, where workers can understand where and how bears use the oil and gas fields. Ultimately, the FWS will have to define the information important to monitoring polar bears and adjust the observation form so it addresses these issues. Bear monitoring programs using observation forms have been implemented by the National Park Service and their forms may be models for FWS polar bear observation forms.

Depending on the activity and the company, daily or monthly logs are kept for the annual report in order to characterize monitoring effort. Some participants expressed the view that they should only report actual sightings of bears, not days when there were no sightings occur, or to provide monthly reports rather than daily when many daily reports show no polar bear observations. This could be accomplished if sample effort integrity is maintained.

Participants noted that monitoring effort for projects varies with the type of activity, i.e., production activities occur throughout the year, compared to exploration activities, which occur in short time periods. FWS needs to standardize this monitoring and reporting data. Certain areas will have a higher probability of observing polar bears. For example, if the operation is far inland it is less likely to see a polar bear. On the other hand, a dedicated bear monitor on a coastal project may see more bears because 1) they may spend more time "actively" monitoring bear activity or 2) because of their location on coastal habitat, they simply have a higher probability of encountering a polar bear due to a bear's preferential use of this habitat.

Annual reports are required from companies and FWS should engage observers to encourage timely submissions of observations and reports. One idea, which has been used by biologists to gather data on polar bears in Norway, is to reward monitors with small prizes, such as lapel pins, to encourage participation.

The FWS needs to provide feedback to participating companies and organizations showing how the information they report is incorporated into polar bear management and conservation. One idea would be teaming up with industry personnel to increase observer training and report feedback. It was noted that there is a need to increase the consistency in the data collected. The goal would be to quantify changes in bear use of the oilfields, by creating consistency with the polar bear information collected on the observation forms. By improving information collection, the FWS should then be able to systematically document increased bear use of the oilfields.

Participants discussed the need to increase training levels of bear monitors in the use of the polar bear observation form. The FWS could improve data input by increasing training in the type of data entry necessary. For example, oilfield security personnel could be given advanced training due to the large amount of data collection they submit to FWS as "first-responders" to bears in the oilfield. In addition, other oilfield personnel could receive polar bear awareness or deterrence training as well in order to receive pertinent information on polar bear use of the oilfields.

<u>Hazing Protocols</u>
Currently, there is an active hazing program on the North Slope through the FWS intentional take program. This involves immediately hazing bears as they move into active developed areas. While hazing is an effective tool to limit polar bear-human interactions, some participants were concerned that the protocol is not appropriate for all bear scenarios. For example, sometimes bears in the late summer reach the coast exhausted from long ocean swims. They show no indication of wanting to move and sometimes do not respond to low-level hazing. If no people are working in the area there may be a possibility to keep the bear under surveillance, rather than hazing the bear (current FWS policy), until it recovers and departs on its own.

Hazing training was traditionally conducted for the oilfield security companies and other contractors that have received incidental and intentional take authorizations. Support companies and contractors, such as drilling and transportation companies (e.g. Catco, Peak, and Crowley Barge), as well as seismic companies that work throughout the Coastal Plain may also need additional polar bear awareness/hazing training because of their large amount of travel in remote coastal areas.

Polar Bear/Human Interaction Recommendations
1. Increase slope-wide information and education programs.
2. Revisit the polar bear hazing protocol as it is related to behavior, i.e., pushing bears vs. letting them rest. More guidance needs to be expressed during certain situations.

3. Staff a FWS position on the North Slope to interface with the oil and gas industry during the time of maximum bear activity.
4. Create a website with current information on incidental take and monitoring of bears on the North Slope.
5. Have meetings with other North Slope operators, groups, and companies (i.e., Catco, Crowley, Peak), rather than just security to promote polar bear awareness and information transfer.
6. Work with other North Slope organizations, such as the NSB, NMFS to promote polar bear awareness and conservation.
7. Discuss with oilfield companies the type of polar bear information necessary for submitting standardized, high-quality observation reports.
8. Overhaul the polar bear observation form.
9. Standardize the LOA issuance process.
10. Enforce LOAs and incidental take violations.
11. Monitor the shipping industry. Future shipping traffic is expected to increase along the arctic coast through polar bear habitat due to global warming that is reducing ice coverage. Managers need to monitor shipping activity and be ready to educate this new user group.

V. RESEARCH VS. MONITORING RECOMMENDATIONS

Comments from participants addressed both research and monitoring. Indeed, most comments during the workshop discussed research needs. Consequently, participants discussed the differences between monitoring and research. Monitoring is a collection of observations, while research addresses specific questions. Monitoring data sets generally become useful as a research tool with multiple years of data. However, managers may not be able to answer broader questions regarding potential effects of industry on polar bears only through monitoring. Monitoring plans must be supported and linked with ongoing research efforts. Well designed and effectively communicated research and monitoring programs will complement each other as managers try to understand anthropogenic effects on polar bears. Monitoring data sets may spur research, while research may lead to better monitoring practices.

Polar bear research-associated recommendations that were considered high priority issues included:
1. Continue research involving population estimation of the Southern Beaufort Sea polar bear stock. Currently, USGS is conducting an ongoing population estimation study.
2. Continue industry support (direct funding and/or logistics) of polar bear research efforts.
3. Consider research studies as cooperative efforts with other federal and state agencies. Several cooperating agencies may make it easier to secure long term outside support and funding.
4. Follow-up the fall coastal polar bear aerial surveys with mark/recapture efforts in order to check accuracy of the aerial survey.
5. Initiate a capture effort program for polar bears in the Chukchi Sea.

6. Develop new technologies, such as radio frequency identification (RFID) tags to use in polar bear research and monitoring.
7. Allow industry to assist in information collection on polar bears in the field (monitoring). Some simple techniques which could be incorporated include hair trap corrals, hair sampling using neck snares, biopsy darts, and captures in the oil fields.
8. Identify the resources necessary to gather the above information (time, money, special equipment).

VI. A MONITORING STRATEGY, AN EVOLVING PROCESS

The basic purpose of monitoring polar bears within the oil and gas fields on the North Slope of Alaska is to establish baseline information on polar bear use and encounters and detect any unforeseen effects of exploration, development, and production activities. Long-term monitoring is necessary to determine the potential impacts of oil and gas activities on polar bears and their habitat over time, and to detect and measure changes in the status of the overall polar bear population in the Beaufort Sea.

As stated earlier, information from this workshop will be used by the FWS to develop a comprehensive, long-term monitoring plan by identifying and prioritizing monitoring tasks, implementing those tasks over time, and updating the monitoring plans periodically. Within these workshop proceedings, recommendations (tasks) have been identified based on potential impacts of the oil and gas industry on polar bears. The impacts discussed were habitat alteration, contamination, attraction and preclusion of areas, oil spills, industrial noise, and polar bear interactions with humans. Recommendations were developed to address these potential impacts; they are not all-encompassing nor will all of the workshop recommendations be implemented. In addition, more recommendations may become apparent as the monitoring plan progresses.

In order to create a workable monitoring plan, the FWS will next evaluate the recommendations of the workshop participants and set priorities. A comprehensive plan would most likely include aspects of monitoring and research and it would incorporate cooperation with various private groups and government agencies. Table 1 is the first step in organizing recommendations discussed during the workshop as tasks to form a monitoring plan. These tasks are set on a 10-year timeline; after which FWS may re-evaluate the impacts affecting polar bears.

Although numerous recommendations were discussed, participants agreed that certain recommendations had a higher priority to implement than others. Some of these recommendations were necessary to lay the groundwork for other tasks. For example, research needs have a high priority where the findings could be used to further advance monitoring and mitigation techniques. On the population level, high priority tasks include continuing research on population estimation of polar bears in the Southern Beaufort Sea stock. Currently, USGS is conducting research in this area. Maintaining funds to continue programs, such as the AMMTAP program, was considered a high priority as well. In addition, solving the bowhead whale carcass pile issues throughout the Arctic coast was also deemed a high priority recommendation.

Additionally, some recommendations will be faster and easier to implement than others, such as improving the polar bear observation form. Other tasks that are easy to implement, but are just as important include having the FWS become more interactive with North Slope personnel on all levels. This would be through outreach and Information and Education programs, as already discussed. Many of these recommendations associated with outreach are easy and relatively fast to implement as they can occur internally in FWS. Regardless of the monitoring approach, some of these recommendations are universal and make good business sense. For example, working closer with North Slope companies and contractors and providing feedback reports to the bear observers that provides information could only improve the working environment between FWS and the operators throughout the oilfields.

A long-term polar bear monitoring program is essential for the future conservation and management of polar bears in Alaska. As human activities increase in the Arctic it will become more important to monitor those activities for possible effects and impacts on polar bears and their habitat and to detect changes to polar bears and their habitat earlier. For this reason, it is necessary for the FWS to work cooperatively with industry regarding polar bear issues. Efforts to minimize industrial effects on polar bears are in everyone's interest. By working together with industry, the FWS will be able to maximize the data-gathering ability of future monitoring programs. Consequently, by preventing potential future problems with the implementation of a sound monitoring program, the FWS will be able to better manage and maintain a healthy polar bear population throughout the Alaskan arctic.

VII. ACKNOWLEDGEMENTS

The FWS would like to thank MMS for funding the workshop (Intra-agency agreement 0102RU85166 NSL # AK 02-06). I would also like to thank all the workshop participants for their time and expertise. Special thanks to Mary Lynn Nation (FWS) and Larry Bright (FWS) for facilitating the workshop. In addition, Scott Schliebe (FWS), the FWS-Marine Mammals Management office, Geoff York (USGS), Steve Amstrup (USGS) and the Alaska Science Center (Polar Bear Group) provided major assistance with the preparation and planning of the workshop and review of the proceedings. I also want to thank Tom Evans and Kelly Proffitt for their logistical support. I shared the draft proceedings with workshop participants and I want to thank Danielle Jerry (FWS), Don Hansen (MMS), Susi Miller (FWS), Chuck Monnett (MMS), Lori Quakenbush (ADFG), Dick Shideler (ADFG), and Geoff York (USGS) for their constructive comments.

Table 1. Polar bear monitoring task schedule. Monitoring components are based on a 10 year projection.

Monitoring Program	Duration	Frequency	Area	Type of Information	Priority[a]
Habitat Alteration Tasks					
Track changes of the physical habitat	ongoing	ongoing	range-wide	Baseline	2
Track habitat changes due to the increased development	ongoing	ongoing	oilfields	Rate	2
Identify polar bear refugia	3-5 years		range-wide	Baseline and distribution	1
Consider the value of restored, abandoned facilities as polar bear habitat, i.e., denning or resting	ongoing	ongoing	oilfields	Baseline and distribution	2
Classify denning habitat in NPR-A and ANWR	3-5 years		NPR-A	Baseline and distribution	1
Monitor arctic climate change data sources	ongoing	ongoing	slope-wide	Baseline	1
Contamination Tasks					
Continue contaminant monitoring archiving program	ongoing	annual	range-wide	Baseline	1
Conduct rigorous analysis of the contaminant data	-	-	-	-	2
Improve sampling protocols and study designs	-	-	-	-	2
Analyze specimens and report results in a timely fashion	-	-	-	-	1
Stabilize funding for the AAMTAP program.	ongoing	annual	range-wide	Supporting	1
Monitor disease and parasites in polar bears	ongoing	annual	range-wide	Baseline	2
Develop a "before/after" monitoring approach	ongoing	5-10 years	site-specific	Rates	3
Attraction/Avoidance Tasks					
Monitor movement of bears from bowhead whale carcass sites to oilfields	3-5 years	carcass-dependent	site-specific	Distribution and Rates	4, 1
Meet with agency, industry, and local governments to discuss the future of whale carcass sites.	-	as needed	regional	Supporting	1
Use industry maps to plot seasonal polar bear locations around oilfield infrastructure	ongoing	with IT Regs	oilfields	Distribution	2

23

Table 1. Polar bear monitoring task schedule. Monitoring components are based on a 10 year projection, continued.

Monitoring Program	Duration	Frequency	Area	Type of Information	Priority[a]
Oil Spill Tasks					
Update and improve precision of oil spill models	1-2 years	with IT regs	regional	Supporting	1
Incorporate polar bear scenarios into North Slope spill drills	-	annual	oilfields	Supporting	1
Update FWS Oil Spill Response Plan	1-2 years	5-10 years	oilfields	Supporting	2
Industrial Noise Tasks					
Revisit the buffer size around maternal polar bear dens: reduce, enlarge, or status quo?	-	with IT regs	oilfields	Behavioral	3
Reassess den mitigation – monitor the den, rather than mitigate around industrial activities	-	with IT regs	oilfields	Behavioral	2
Human Interaction Tasks					
Increase information and education programs (Outreach)	ongoing	annual	slope-wide	Supporting	1
Overhaul the polar bear observation form	-	5 years	oilfields	Baseline, Distribution, Rates	1
Revisit polar bear hazing protocol: pushing bears vs. letting them rest	-	-	site-specific - LOA dependent	Behavioral	2
Increase FWS presence on the North Slope	ongoing	seasonal	slope-wide	Supporting	1
Create a website for current polar bear information	ongoing	seasonal	range-wide	Supporting	3
Increase polar bear awareness training to North Slope operators, groups, and companies	ongoing	annual	oilfields	Supporting	4
Work with other North Slope organizations (NSB, NMFS) for polar bear conservation	ongoing	as needed	slope-wide	Supporting	4
Meet with oilfield security about the type of information necessary to be collected.	-	1-3 years	oilfields	Supporting	2
Standardize the LOA issuance process	-	with IT regs	oilfields	Supporting	4
Enforce LOAs and incidental take violations	-	with IT regs	oilfields	Supporting	1
Monitor the annual numbers of polar bear-viewing tourists	seasonal	annual	regional	Baseline	2
Monitor the arctic shipping industry	seasonal	annual	range-wide	Baseline	3

Table 1. Polar bear monitoring task schedule. Monitoring components are based on a 10 year projection, continued.

Monitoring Program	Duration	Frequency	Area	Type of Information	Priority[a]
Research Tasks					
Continue research involving population estimation of the Southern Beaufort Sea polar bear stock	3-5 years	5-10 years	range-wide	Population estimate	1
Continue industry support of polar bear population estimation efforts	ongoing	annual	range-wide	Population estimate	1
Consider research studies as cooperative efforts with other federal and state agencies	ongoing	ongoing	range-wide	Supporting	2
Follow-up the fall coastal polar bear aerial surveys with mark/recapture efforts	survey-dependent	once	range-wide	Baseline, Distribution, Rate	2
Initiate a capture effort program for polar bears in the Chukchi Sea	3-5 years	5-10 years	range-wide	Baseline, Distribution, Rates, Population estimation	3
Compare denning on human-created substrates to surrounding natural areas	3-5 years	once	range-wide	Behavioral	3
Design a study to test disturbance to female bears in dens	3-5 years	once	range-wide	Behavioral	2
Develop new technologies to use in polar bear research and monitoring.	ongoing	ongoing	range-wide	Comprehensive	1
Predict the use of sea ice vs. terrestrial maternal denning habitat	3-5 years	once	range-wide	Behavioral	3
Allow industry to assist in field information collection on polar bears (monitoring)	ongoing	ongoing	oilfields	Supporting	2
Identify the resources necessary to accomplish the research projects	ongoing	ongoing	oilfields	Supporting	1

Priority Rating
[a] 1 = High: Implement as soon as possible
2 = Moderate: Implement in near future 3-5 years
3 = Low: Implement in future >5 years
4 = Currently implemented, needs improvements

25

APPENDIX 1.

Attendees of the Beaufort Sea Polar Bear Monitoring Workshop

Attendees of the Beaufort Sea Polar Bear Monitoring Workshop

3-5 September 2003

Steve Amstrup
USGS
Alaska Science Center
1011 E. Tudor Rd.
Anchorage, AK 99503
907/786-3424
steven_amstrup@usgs.gov

Gene Augustine
611 CES/CEVP
10471 20th St., Rm 336
Elmendorf AFB, AK 99506-2200
gene.augustine@elmendorf.af.mil

Larry Bright
USFWS
101 12th Ave., Box 19
Fairbanks, AK 99701
907/456-0324
larry_bright@fws.gov

Robert Buchanan
Polar Bears International
35555 Spur Hwy, #320
Soldotna, AK 99669
907/252-8525
Robearbuck@aol.com

Deena Clayton
EnCana Corp.
150 9th Ave. SW
Calgary, Alberta
403/645-5736
deena.clayton@encana.com

Karen Deatherage
Defenders of Wildlife
308 G St. # 310
Anchorage, AK 99501
907/276-9453
defenders@alaska.net

Andrew Derocher
University of Alberta
Biological Sciences
CW405, Edmonton, Alberta
T6G2E9
780/492-5570
derocher@ualberta.ca

George Durner
USGS
Alaska Science Center
1011 E. Tudor Rd.
Anchorage, AK 99503
907/786-3366
george_durner@usgs.gov

Allison J. Erickson
OASIS Environmental
BP Environmental Studies
807 G St., Suite 250
Anchorage, AK 99501
907/258-4880
Allison@oasisenviro.com

Tom Evans
U.S. Fish and Wildlife Service
Marine Mammals Management
1011 E. Tudor Road
Anchorage, AK 99503
907/786-3814
tom_evans@fws.gov

Don Hansen
Minerals Management Service
3801 Centerpoint Drive, Suite 500
Anchorage, AK 99503
(907) 271-6656
Don.Hansen@mms.gov

John Hechtel
Alaska Dept. of Fish and Game
1800 Glenn Hwy, Suite 4
Palmer, AK 99645
907/746-6331
john_hechtel@fishgame.state.ak.us

Danielle Jerry
U.S. Fish and Wildlife Service
1011 E. Tudor Road
Anchorage, AK 99503
907/786-3335
danielle_jerry@fws.gov

Susi (Kalxdorff) Miller
U.S. Fish and Wildlife Service
Marine Mammals Management
1011 E. Tudor Road
Anchorage, AK 99503
907/786-3828
susanne_miller@fws.gov

Todd Logan
U.S. Fish and Wildlife Service
1011 E. Tudor Road
Anchorage, AK 99503
907/786-3667
todd_logan@fws.gov

Trent McDonald
West, Inc
2003 Central Ave.
Cheyenne, WY 82001
307/634-1756
tmcdonald@west-inc.com

Rosa Meehan
U.S. Fish and Wildlife Service
Marine Mammals Management
1011 E. Tudor Road
Anchorage, AK 99503
907/786-3349
rosa_meehan@fws.gov

Pamela A. Miller
Arctic Connections
P.O. Box 101811
Anchorage, AK 99510
907/272-1909
pammiller@alaska.com

Chuck Monnett
Mineral Management Service
3801 Centerpoint Drive, Suite 500
Anchorage, AK 99503
(907) 271-6677
charles.monnett@mms.gov

John Nagy
Department of Resources, Wildlife, and
Economic Development
Bag Service #1
Inuvik, NT
X0E 0T0
867/777-7236
john_nagy@gov.nt.ca

Mary Lynn Nation
U.S. Fish and Wildlife Service
1011 E. Tudor Road
Anchorage, AK 99503
907/786-3519
marylynn_nation@fws.gov

David Nyland
Western GeCo
351 E. International Airport Rd.
Anchorage, AK 99518
907/550-3542
physics@mtaonline.net

Lori Quakenbush
Alaska Department of Fish and Game
1300 College Rd.
Fairbanks, Alaska 99701
907/459-7214
lori_quakenbush@fishgame.state.ak.us

Craig Perham
U.S. Fish and Wildlife Service
Marine Mammals Management
1011 E. Tudor Road
Anchorage, AK 99503
907/786-3810
craig_perham@fws.gov

Caryn Rea
ConocoPhillips
700 G St.
P.O. Box 100360
Anchorage, AK 99510
907/265-6515
caryn.rea@conocophillips.com

Lisa Rotterman
Minerals Management Service
3801 Centerpoint Drive, Suite 500
Anchorage, AK 99503
(907) 271-6604
Lisa.rotterman@mms.gov

Glenn Ruckhaus
Lynx Enterprises, Inc.
1029 W. 3rd Ave. #400
Anchorage, AK 99507
907/277-4611
gruckhaus@lynxalaska.com

Scott Schliebe
U.S. Fish and Wildlife Service
Marine Mammals Management
1011 E. Tudor Road
Anchorage, AK 99503
907/786-3812
scott_schliebe@fws.gov

John Schoen
The Audubon Society
308 G St.
Anchorage, AK
907/276-7034
jschoen@audubon.org

Dick Shideler
Alaska Department of Fish and Game
1300 College Rd.
Fairbanks, Alaska 99701
907/459-7283
dick_shideler@fishgame.state.ak.us

Kristen Simac
USGS
Alaska Science Center
1011 E. Tudor Rd.
Anchorage, AK 99503
907/786-3928
kristen_simac@usgs.gov

Tom Smith
USGS
Alaska Biological Center
1011 E. Tudor Rd.
Anchorage, AK 99503
907/786-3456
tom_smith@usgs.gov

Bill Streever
BP Exploration (Alaska) Inc.
P.O. Box 196612
Anchorage, AK 99519
907/564-4383
streevbj@bp.com

Dave Trudgen
OASIS Environmental
807 G St., Suite 250
Anchorage, AK 99501
907/258-4880
Dave@oasisenviro.com

Holly Wheeler
Department of Interior
Solicitor's Office
Washington D.C.
202/208-5233

Geoff York
USGS
Alaska Science Center
1011 E. Tudor Rd.
Anchorage, AK 99503
907/786-3928
geoff_york@usgs.gov

APPENDIX 2.

Agenda of Polar Bear Monitoring Workshop

Beaufort Sea Polar Bear Monitoring Workshop

3-5 September 2003

Location: Hilltop Ski Area Lodge
               Anchorage, Alaska

Purpose of the Workshop: Facilitate the evaluation and discussion necessary to identify components to develop a comprehensive monitoring program for polar bears in relation to the oil and gas industry in Alaska.

Goal: This workshop will be the initial effort to design an effective monitoring strategy that will provide information to help reduce bear/human interactions and help protect polar bear habitat for the Southern Beaufort Sea polar bear population.

Product: An improved management plan identifying types of information necessary to monitor polar bears thereby helping USFWS better manage the Southern Beaufort Sea polar bear population.

DAY 1 (WEDNESDAY, 3 SEPTEMBER 2003)   8:30 AM TO 4:45 PM

8:00 am	**Registration**
8:30 am	**Introduction**
	Objectives/Expected product
9:00 am - 9:30 am	**Recent Population Estimate** *Steve Amstrup, ASC, USGS*
9:30 am - 10:00 am	**Distribution of polar bear denning in Alaska determined by satellite radio telemetry** *Steve Amstrup, ASC, USGS*
10:00 am - 10:15 am	**Break**
10:15 am - 10:45 am	**The use of sea ice habitat by polar bears in the Beaufort Sea** *George Durner, ASC, USGS*

1

10:45 am - 11:15 am	**Aerial Surveys of polar bears along the coast and barrier islands of the Beaufort Sea** *Scott Schliebe, Marine Mammals Management, USFWS*
11:15 am - 11:45 am	**Polar Bear Use of Marine Mammal Carcasses in the Central Beaufort Sea** *Susi Kalxdorf, Marine Mammals Management, USFWS*
11:45 am - 1:00 pm	Lunch
1:00 pm - 1:30 pm	**Assessment of industrial sounds and vibrations received in artificial dens** *Mike Williams, LGL Alaska Research Associates, Inc.*
1:30 pm - 2:00 pm	**Post-emergence observations of polar bears at den sites in Northern Alaska** *Tom Smith, ASC, USGS*

MITIGATION TOOLS FROM RECENT RESEARCH EFFORTS:

2:00 pm - 2:30 pm	**Terrestrial maternal den site characteristics** *George Durner, ASC, USGS*
2:30 pm - 3:00 pm	**Detecting denning polar bears with forward looking infrared imagery (FLIR)** *Geoff York, ASC, USGS*
3:00 pm - 3:30 pm	**The use of trained dogs to verify polar bear den occupancy** *Mike Williams, LGL Alaska Research Associates, Inc.*
3:30 pm - 3:45 pm	Break
3:45 pm - 4:15 pm	**Marine Mammal Monitoring program, McCovey exploration prospect, Winter 2002-03** *Glen Ruckhaus, Lynx Enterprises, Inc.*
4:15 pm - 4:45 pm	**Summary of Incidental and Intentional Take of polar bears during oil and gas industry operations in the Beaufort Sea region of Alaska** *Craig Perham, Marine Mammals Management, USFWS*
4:45 pm	**Comments and Adjournment**

DAY 2 (THURSDAY 4 SEPTEMBER 2003) 8:30 AM TO 4:30 PM

WORKING GROUP SESSION

8:00 am   **Registration and refreshments**

8:30 am   **Introduction to working group structure; goals and objectives for working group; expected product**

9:00 am – 10:30 am   **Habitat alteration**   Discussion Leader: George Durner

10:30 am - 10:45 am   **Break**

10:45 am - 11:45 am   **Contaminants**   Discussion Leader: Andy Derocher

11:45 am - 1:00 pm   **Lunch**

1:00 pm - 2:00 pm   **Attraction/preclusion**   Discussion Leader: Dick Shideler

2:00 pm - 2:15 pm   **Break**

2:15 pm - 4:00 pm   **Oil Spill**   Discussion Leader: Steve Amstrup

4:00 pm - 4:30 pm   **Comments and Daily Wrap-up**

DAY 3 (FRIDAY 5 SEPTEMBER 2003) 8:15 AM TO 12:00 PM

Continue with Working Group Meeting (if necessary)

8:15 am - 9:30 am   Noise   Discussion Leader: Mike Williams

9:30 am - 9:45 am   Break

9:45 am - 11:00 am   Human interaction (lethal/nonlethal)   Discussion Leader: Scott Schliebe

11:00 am - 12:00 pm   Workshop Wrap-up

End product: Information to compile into a draft report

APPENDIX 3.

Current Polar Bear Observation Form

United States Department of the Interior

FISH AND WILDLIFE SERVICE
1011 E. Tudor Road
Anchorage, Alaska 99503-6199

POLAR BEAR SIGHTING REPORT

Date:_____
Time:_____

Location: (include GPS coordinates if possible)_____
_____

Observer name:_____

Weather conditions: Fog_____ Snow_____ Rain_____ Clear_____ Approx. temperature_____

Wind speed_____ Wind direction_____

Total number of bears: Sow/cubs_____ Adult_____ Sub-adult_____ Unknown_____

Estimated distance of bear(s) from personnel/facility:_____

Possible attractants present:_____

Bear behavior: Curious_____ Aggressive_____ Predatory_____ Other_____

Description of encounter:_____
_____
_____

Duration of encounter:_____

Deterrents used/distance: Vehicle_____ Noise-maker_____ Firearms_____ Other_____

Injuries sustained: Personnel:_____
                        Polar bear:_____

Agency/Contacts:

USFWS_____ Time_____Date_____
ADF&G_____ Time_____Date_____
CLIENT_____ Time_____Date_____

The Department of the Interior Mission

As the Nation's principal conservation agency, the Department of the Interior has responsibility for most of our nationally owned public lands and natural resources. This includes fostering sound use of our land and water resources; protecting our fish, wildlife, and biological diversity; preserving the environmental and cultural values of our national parks and historical places; and providing for the enjoyment of life through outdoor recreation. The Department assesses our energy and mineral resources and works to ensure that their development is in the best interest of all our people by encouraging stewardship and citizen participation in their care. The Department also has a major responsibility for American Indian reservation communities and for people who live in island territories under U.S. administration.

The Minerals Management Service Mission

As a bureau of the Department of the Interior, the Minerals Management Service's (MMS) primary responsibilities are to manage the mineral resources located on the Nation's Outer Continental Shelf (OCS), collect revenue from the Federal OCS and onshore Federal and Indian lands, and distribute those revenues.

Moreover, in working to meet its responsibilities, the **Offshore Minerals Management Program** administers the OCS competitive leasing program and oversees the safe and environmentally sound exploration and production of our Nation's offshore natural gas, oil and other mineral resources. The MMS **Royalty Management Program** meets its responsibilities by ensuring the efficient, timely and accurate collection and disbursement of revenue from mineral leasing and production due to Indian tribes and allottees, States and the U.S. Treasury.

The MMS strives to fulfill its responsibilities through the general guiding principles of: (1) being responsive to the public's concerns and interests by maintaining a dialogue with all potentially affected parties and (2) carrying out its programs with an emphasis on working to enhance the quality of life for all Americans by lending MMS assistance and expertise to economic development and environmental protection.

www.ingramcontent.com/pod-product-compliance
Lightning Source LLC
Chambersburg PA
CBHW080925290526
45795CB00007BA/2658